Contents

Preface   2

Chapter 1 - Take A Lesson   5

Chapter 2 - What's In The Bag?   7

Chapter 3 - Wedges   13

Chapter 4 - Choose Your Budget   18

Chapter 5 - Look After Your Clubs   21

Chapter 6 - Golf Takes Balls   24

Chapter 7 - Golf Fitness   26

Chapter 8 - Putt For Dough   30

Chapter 9 - Green Reading Routine   32

Chapter 10 -Putting Distance Routine   35

Chapter 11 - Golf & Wellbeing   38

Preface

In my opinion, there's no game quite like golf, for me, and millions of others, it's the best sport in the world. Not only do you have the excitement, drama and tension when watching as a spectator. But as a player, you also get unprecedented access to the world's top courses, and the chance to emulate your heroes. The access you get to top golf courses is unlike any other sport. You won't be able to play a backhand winner on Centre Court at Wimbledon, like Roger Federer.

It's also unlikely that you'll get the chance to make a buzzer-beater shot at the United Centre, in the style of Michael Jordan.

However, you can walk across the Swilcan Bridge at St Andrews on your way to the 18th green. You can even attempt to emulate Constantino Rocca's miraculous 65-foot putt from the Valley of Sin to win the 1995 Open Championship. No golf course has hosted more Open tournaments than St Andrews. As a golfer

you not only get the chance to watch this amazing competition, but you can even play the course and walk the same fairways as the legends of the game.

It's easy to see why so many people fall in love with golf, for this reason alone. However, the appeal of golf is not just to do with access, it's also the chance to spend a few hours walking among some of the most beautiful surroundings in the world. Also, golf is truly a sport for all ages, you may well have heard of a golfer in their nineties, who defies general medical opinion by playing a round every week. (and probably shooting a decent score). Then I have no doubt that when you're scanning social media you've come across a video posted by a proud parent of their young child hitting a hole in one, or smashing a driver down the middle of the fairway.

So, for many reasons this is an amazing game. Yes, golf does have the image of only being for the elite or wealthy, this can be true when you look at golf equipment costs or some club membership fees. However, this image is changing. The profile of today's top professional golfers is helping to reinforce this change. Take PGA Professional Andrew 'Beef' Johnston, he grew up in London in a working-class family, his dad was a bus driver and his mother a dinner lady. Despite this he has been able to make it to the top of this game.

Golf is a mentally challenging game, with no two rounds the same. The game's object is to complete 18 holes by hitting the golf ball from the teeing area towards the green in the fewest number of strokes. How one golfer does this will vary from how another plays the same 18 holes, you can have your own style, and be completely unique in how you play.

To get the most from this amazing sport though, you will need to spend some time learning the fundamentals of the game from the beginning. Doing this will prevent you from following the same path as golfers who struggle to improve and enjoy the game. This will help you reap the rewards in the future.

This book came about from my desire to help beginner golfers and those who want to learn more about the game get the best start in golf. I will explore some of the fundamentals of the game and will also offer you tips and advice to improve your golf. Let's face it when you can play golf effectively, a trip to the golf course is much more fun, and it's always great if you can beat your playing partners.

You never know, if you follow these tips, practice effectively, and it could be you hitting the course record at the Old Course at St Andrews in the near future!

Chapter 1 - Take A Lesson

In every top sport, world class players seek professional help and have a coach to help them with their game. Golf is not different, watch any practice range at a PGA tournament and you'll see the pros spending time under the watchful eye of their golf coach. If it's a good idea for the top players, then it's definitely a good idea for the average golfer.

The one thing every golfer on the course has in common is the desire to hit longer drives and shoot lower scores. In such a technical sport, with so many intricacies affecting the swing and the strike of the ball, if you want to improve your golf, taking a lesson can help you achieve this goal.

Paying for professional golf lessons with a PGA Pro not only means that you are serious about your game, but it also means that you are almost guaranteed to improve your golf, if you stick with it. Golf lessons are essential if you want to play better golf. Not only do you receive one-on-one instruction from a pro who knows how to improve your golf swing, they can also help you pick out the right clubs, learn how to manage your short game, and get the ball in the hole.

Tips to get the most from your golf lessons:

1.　Decide what you want to achieve from your lessons. Is there a particular part of your game you want to improve, long game, short game, putting? If you plan this in advance you will get more out of your lessons.

2.　Be honest with your instructor, don't pretend that you're better than you are. Firstly, they'll tell straight away, and secondly the more honest you are with them the better your relationship will be. This will help both of you get the most out of your time together.

3.　Be clear on what specific actions you should be working on following your lesson. Don't let there be any ambiguity with what you should be practicing on in the time until your next lesson.

4.　Finally, don't take lessons from your friends, or your spouse, it won't end well!

Chapter 2 - What's In The Bag?

If you are reading this, I'm sure you are familiar with the different types of golf clubs used in playing the game. However, let's just take some time to review this area.

An average golfer's bag contains a variety of different clubs, each designed with a specific purpose in mind for playing. The names of the typical golf clubs used in the game of golf are woods, wedges, irons and a putter.

Iron clubs generally come in numbers three to nine iron, not including wedges which are explained further below, they are used to cover medium distances between 215 and 130 yards. Modern golf sets however make use of Fairway woods and hybrid clubs, in place of the lower numbered irons as these are generally more forgiving, versatile and easier to hit.

In the past golfers would have used irons numbered 1-3 for the longer approach shots onto the green as opposed to the fairway woods. These longer irons are notoriously difficult to hit with.

Golfer Lee Trevino, when asked about the difficulty of the 1 iron, was famously quoted as saying:

"If your caught in a storm and are afraid of lightning, hold up a 1 iron. Even God can't hit a 1 iron"

The numbers on the bottom of clubs provide an easy way for golfers to identify which clubs they should select for their shot. They distinguish the degree of loft the clubs have. The higher numbers have a higher degree of loft and the lower numbers have a lower degree of loft and carry the ball longer distances. For example, the 5 iron which has a loft of 27 degrees will have an average yardage of 160 yards. It is designed to hit the ball a longer distance and take the ball flight over a lower height trajectory. In contrast the 9 iron has a club loft of 42 degrees and will have an average yardage of 120 yards, but the ball will have a much higher flight path due to the amount of loft on the club face and it will take a shorter amount of distance for the ball to reach its maximum height trajectory.

I've included a helpful golf club distance chart. This will help guide you to the differences between the loft and the distances

Golf Tips - How To Improve Your Golf

of the clubs in your golf bag:

	Ave. Yardage	Club Loft	Club Length
Driver	250	10°	45"
3 Wood	210	13°	43"
5 Wood	190	17°	41.5"
Hybrid	175	23°	39"
5 Iron	160	27°	38"
6 Iron	150	30°	37.5"
7 Iron	140	34°	37"
8 Iron	130	38°	36.5"
9 Iron	120	42°	36"
Pitching Wedge	110	46°	35.5"
Gap Wedge	100	50°	35.25"
Sand Wedge	85	56°	35"
Lob Wedge	70	60°	35"

The Driver is one of the most difficult clubs to hit, mainly due to the length of the club and the distance you are standing away from the ball. Therefore, we see that this alone can provide a larger margin for error with this club. When choosing a driver to buy, you need to make sure you've had the chance to practice with it first in the first place. Many golf shops and outlets will allow this, either in the indoor swing analysis studio or on the nearby practice range.

Golfers love to hit long distances; the driver is the perfect club

that delivers these greater distances. With advances in technology, the golf drivers nowadays can hit incredibly long distances. The club heads are made from metal alloys or advanced materials. These clubs remain to be referred to as 'woods' though, even though the material has evolved away from wooden material.

During the last few years, several manufacturers of golf equipment have adopted the technology of adjustable drivers that allow players to set up various attributes of the club to make it more customized. The adjustable drivers enable a golfer to vary the loft angles across wide ranges, adjust angle of the club face, lie angle, and the gravitational centre of your club head.

There are some important things for a beginner golfer to consider when choosing a golf driver. I've listed below some of the tips you should be aware of when making your choice.

The head size of drivers does matter. If you have just begun to play golf beginners should use drivers with a large 460cc club head, it's the maximum permissible size in the USGA rules of golf. Drivers with bigger club heads can help you improve your golf to a great extent due to the 'sweet spot' being larger and providing a better chance of the ball going in the right direction, even with shots slightly off centre.

When choosing the perfect driver, you must also pair the driver with the correct club shaft.

This relates to how flexible the shaft of the club will be when you complete the swing. If you have a slower swing speed. Maybe for beginners, juniors, or women golfers, you might be better off with a regular flex club shaft.

There is also the option of a stiff or extra stiff shaft flex which makes the shaft less flexible when being swung, this is designed for golfers with a faster swing speed.

Have a look at the chart below to provide some insight into how swing speed affects the type of club flex you'll require.

Shot Distance	Clubhead Speed	Shaft Flex
180 to 200 yards	75 to 85 mph	Senior
200 to 240 yards	85 to 95 mph	Regular
240 to 275 yards	95 to 110 mph	Stiff/Firm

Fairway Woods, these clubs have a head that is slightly smaller than the driver and have a higher degree of loft. They are designed for hitting the golf ball longer distances off the ground to cover distances of between 180 – 220 yards depending on the club type, and your skill level.

Fairway woods can have a big impact on your game by allowing

you to easily hit the ball to the green or surrounding area from a longer distance from the fairway or the rough. The design of these clubs mean that they are generally easier to hit than the longer irons, and for this reason have become a regular part of golfers' bags.

Hybrids, not to be confused with fairway woods, are also excellent for beginners. With longer irons so hard to hit for beginner golfer's hybrid golf clubs have become increasingly popular.

The small club face and low club trajectory for these types of clubs make them better to hit from both the fairway and the rough. As these are generally easier to hit and more forgiving for the beginner golfer. Some golf equipment companies have produced hybrid versions of their entire set from long irons all the way to wedges.

Chapter 3 - Wedges

There are four main classes of wedge, and each has its own strengths and abilities. We've detailed these below but firstly let's explain a little more about wedges.

Gene Sarazen, an American professional golfer during the 1930's and 40's is widely credited with inventing the style for the modern wedge. In the past the irons used in the bunkers and around the green would have very little loft and be more of a blade style club. This made it difficult to get under the ball in the sand and allow the ball to stop on the green without running. Sarazen developed his wedge using the equivalent of a 9 iron and giving it a higher degree of loft, he also built it up under the base of the club to allow a better swing through sand or grass.

This club assisted Sarazen on his way to winning Major golf tournaments in Britain and America.

The different types of golf wedges that exist might look very

similar in their features and technology, but they are not. Understanding the different types and specifications of a golf wedge is vital to get the most out of your game.

The four main classes of wedge are the **Pitching Wedge, Gap Wedge, Sand Wedge and Lob Wedge.**
The key to choosing the best golf wedge for beginners is to ensure that there is no large gap between the loft of each club.

Pitching Wedge

Abbreviated as PW, the modern pitching wedge hits the ball the farthest of the different types of wedge. The pitching wedge has a lower loft angle between 46 to 48 degrees. The low loft of the pitching wedge makes the ball fly a bit lower in the air and roll farther when it lands on the green. In other words, Golfers use this wedge to hit a long-distance shot.
A pitching wedge is considered indispensable and it is meant to be carried around always. The Pitching wedge is generally used from the fairway or the rough to approach the green from distances of approximately 100-120 yards.
As with other types of wedge club this can also be used

effectively to chip up onto the green from shorter distances and allow the ball to roll after landing in a chip and run.

Gap Wedge

This is the best golf wedge to use when trying to bring your ball closer to the flag for high performance and reliability. This club was created to bridge the loft gap between pitching wedge and sand wedge, which can have up to 10 degrees in difference. These gap wedge clubs are generally 50-52 degrees and allow skilled players to be able to effectively find the right club to get as close to the flag from between 100-80 yards. The popularity of this club is the way that it has bridged the gap between the pitching wedge and the sand wedge. It has been designed to be able to be used in the sand but also being well designed enough to easily hit from the fairway.

Sand Wedge

The sand wedge, as the name might suggest, is designed to be used in sand bunkers. The sand wedge is used to easily exit sand bunkers. It is the widest of all the golf wedges. It offers the best club shape to allow the head to pass through the sand smoothly and avoid digging.

The sand wedge can also be especially useful in hard, moist, soft long grass, and is also used effectively on loose ground or wood chips. It has a higher club loft, averaging 56 degrees and has a high bounce angle meaning this is perfect for bunker shots, but not great from a flat bare lie.

Lob Wedge

The lob wedge was made famous by 'Flop Master' Phil Mickelson. The lob wedge lifts the ball with a loft of 60 degrees.

These tactical shots are great when you must land the ball on an elevated green with risks on all sides, and you just need to land it softly with little or no roll.

This club is ideal in situations where you have a limited landing area. Mickelson performs an amazing trick shot by placing someone a few yards in front of him, before hitting a full lob wedge flop shot and making the ball loop straight up in the air and over the top of the person's head before safely landing be- hind them on the ground. Shot making at its best.

This club became popular in the early 1980's by Tom Kite it was in response to more difficult green designs which made landing the ball on the green more difficult. These clubs can also be hit from approximately 70-80 yards distance but are far more effective in and around the green.

There are clubs which have been produced which have even more loft than the lob wedge, some named the 'ultra-lob wedge', or the 'flop wedge', these marketing stunts have loft in the region of 70 degrees.

There seems to be little use for these when you can effectively open up the lob wedge if necessary and many have dismissed these as gimmicks.

Wedge Tips:

1.   Be confident, lots of amateurs slow the swing at the point of impact, trying to have a softer control of the shot, or maybe have nerves about hitting it wrong. This can lead to duffing or blading shots. The only way to have the best contact and hit the ball clean is to be confident in your swing. Turn the body, swing through with your arms during your follow through, so that your upper body has turned facing towards the target. This way you will have a clean shot every time and improve your golf score.

2.   When chipping the ball from a short distance onto the green aim to limit the movement in your lower body. Try and turn just your arms and chest, much like a putting stroke. However, be sure not to be too rigid in your wrists. Used effectively you will utilise the loft in the club and get the ball close to the hole each time.

Chapter 4 - Choose Your Budget

There are some golfers who will max out on golf clubs and buy brand new, top of the range equipment, spending thousands, before even hitting their first golf ball. This is fine for some, but as enthusiastic as you may be, to go and spend big on your new hobby buying the most expensive clubs won't make you perform better. Unless you have been playing for a while and have fully committed to the game, I'd really encourage you to think about investing in pre-owned clubs. However, even the experienced golfer can find a gem amongst the many options for pre-owned clubs.

With some targeted research on the Internet you can easily find some excellent brands that will suit your golfing needs. Buying second-hand golf clubs can be good for your budget so that you don't overspend. Don't be afraid of buying golf clubs that have been pre-loved as long as you don't exceed your budget. My first advice would be that after discovering your playing levels, set a budget you can adhere to then you will be ready to move on to the next step of choosing golf clubs, knowing what to look for.

When buying shoes do you just pick the first ones you see on the shelf, or do you have your feet measured and then choose the pair which will fit you the best? Choosing the wrong size shoes might be fine for a while, but over time they will give you problems with your posture, cause you pain, and no doubt cause blisters.

In a similar way, if you simply select off the shelf clubs, they could also cause you long term problems with your game. Initially they might be fine, but if the loft, lie and length of the clubs are incompatible with your body type and swing, they could cause you problems and hold back your progression.

I would recommend you get a professional assessment of what type of clubs you need. You can get this club check assessment for free at many golf pro shops, or golf superstores. They will give you an expert breakdown of how your height, posture and movement will determine what type of club set-up you require. Once armed with this information you can now get back to the internet, or golf shops and find the perfect match for your next set of clubs.

Tips for choosing pre-owned clubs:

1.   Watch out for wedges. Over time, with heavy use, the grooves on some wedges can get badly worn which will affect the spin generated from your shots. This could negatively impact your scores.

2.   Don't be put off by poor or worn grips. These can easily be changed, and sometimes simply replacing a grip can breathe new life into any age club.

3.   Putters can be a real opportunity. With most putters only getting light use, (unless they've been regularly three putting), even older putters can still have a lot of life left in them. These can be perfect to watch out for when you're searching for your pre-owned clubs.

Chapter 5 - Look After Your Clubs

No matter what level of golfer you are and however much money you will have spent on your set of clubs, you should make sure that you take good care of your clubs. Golf clubs can be broken down into three sections: The head, the shaft, and the grip; there are ways to ensure each part stays in top condition, and things you should avoid if you want your clubs to last a long time.

Tips On Looking After Your Golf Clubs

For all parts of your golf clubs, you can use warm water with a household detergent - washing up liquid is ideal.

1. The golf club head.

The golf club head must be kept clean, this is the only part of the club that actually makes contact with the ball. Any dirt or debris in the grooves can affect the strike, even with a putter. Also, if you keep playing with dirt in the grooves, it could even damage them.

When playing your round, you should ensure that each clubhead is wiped after your shots. However, routinely you should take time to give your clubs a deeper clean.

For the club heads use a soft scrubbing brush with the warm soapy water, gently scrub the clubhead, paying particular attention to those grooves. Rinse the clubhead with clean water, and then dry the head with a soft cloth or towel. This is important; otherwise, you may start seeing rust spots - especially if you've owned your clubs for a while.

2. The shaft.

During your round, the most important thing with the metal shafts is to dry them if they've got wet. Otherwise, you may find rust spots developing. The other important thing (including graphite shafts) is to wipe them down to remove any grit that may have got on them as you've put clubs back into your golf bag. This is to ensure they don't get scratched.

3. The grip.

A good condition (and clean) grip should feel slightly 'tacky,' especially when you are wearing the right glove. It's essential to keep your grips in good condition; otherwise the club might slip in your hands during your swing. This could prove

disastrous for your golf score.

To maintain your grips, again, use warm soapy water but use a scouring pad or stiff brush and give a proper scrub. Rinse them afterwards with clean water and then dry with a towel or leave to air dry.

On a final note about the golf club grips, your grips should be replaced regularly, including your putter grip, depending upon how much you play. If you're playing 1-2 times a week your grips will probably last up to 12 months, this will take a reasonable amount of practice time into consideration. If you're playing 3-4 times a week you might need to change your grips after around 6 months. Take this into consideration with how regularly you should change your grips.

4. Use a cover for your putter.

Your 'woods' (driver / 3-wood) will come with covers to protect them, and perhaps your putter will. If it doesn't, see if you can buy one - you use your putter more frequently than any other club, and you need to protect the clubhead.

The most important tip for all golfers, listen carefully. Don't use iron head covers, this is wrong on so many levels, and is a real golf fashion faux pas, just don't do it!

Golf Tips - How To Improve Your Golf

Chapter 6 - Golf Takes Balls

If you want to improve your game, you need to ensure you choose the right golf balls. Golf ball technology has advanced so much that there is debate now if there is too much of an advantage to the PGA professional, and helping their game too much. For us amateurs however let's take every advantage we can get to reduce our score.

At first golf balls seem like a secondary element in the game of golf but, these little things play an important role. The golf balls you see today didn't have this shape and design up until 1900. The first golf ball was made from wood back in the 14th century. Obviously, you can expect the ball to not be perfectly round because these were made by hand and carpenter tools. Then in the 1700s' the designers redefined golf balls by using a leather outlet filled with bird feathers. There were some drawbacks, for example, these versions behaved differently in ranging weather and didn't have a perfectly round shape.

Then came the era where balls were made with moulds. Moulded balls were the brainchild of Robert Addams Paterson. He discovered when sap from sapodilla tree is heated and placed
in mould, it takes the shape of that specific mould. The makers named the ball Guttie and its success raged all over the world. People started mass-manufacturing the Guttie. Different elements were placed in Guttie to make it more stable and carving was done to increase the aerodynamics of the ball. After Guttie's success, in 1890, a new type was created when Coburn Haskell visited B.F Goodrich Rubber Good Manufactory. Coburn and Bertram designed the rubber golf ball. Since then this type of design is still used. To date, many modifications have been made to golf balls and now, millions of manufacturers are working tirelessly to make the best golf ball.

Of all types of golf ball, soft golf balls are generally considered an excellent ball for a newer golfer. They contain a lower compression rate, and they are recommended if you are a beginner. It has been shown in studies that softer golf balls go further while assuring maximum control and lower drag. Essentially what this gives the high handicap golfer is maximum distance with a durable ball which offers good control around the green. All this coming at a very affordable price, particularly important when high handicappers lose a dozen balls every round.

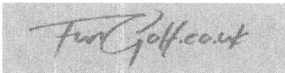

Chapter 7 - Golf Fitness

Many people forget that golf is a physical sport that requires training and conditioning.

While the uninitiated think that golf is a game requiring little physical prowess, experienced players know better. When it comes to playing a round and doing it well, the game demands strength, endurance, and flexibility. A golf fitness workout is a must to accomplish these things.

A good golf workout plan involves a routine that is followed diligently off the green. So, if you want to drive the ball 300 yards, a fitness plan and some strength training can help.

In my research for this book I was lucky enough to catch up with Nick Buchan, Owner/Head Coach of Stronger Golf. Nick is a Titleist Performance Institute (TPI) certified strength coach with a passion for getting golfers stronger and moving better. Through Stronger Golf he uses unique, research-based training methods to create stronger, faster, more athletic golfers. Golfers who are more coachable, achieve higher levels of skill mastery, play injury free, and for longer, because of improved physical fitness.

What I hadn't considered as a low mid-handicapper is how my fitness and conditioning is holding back my progress, limiting my ability to hit longer drives, and increasing my chances of injury.

Nick explained that 80% of golf injuries are through overuse. The most common golf injuries are those involving the lower back and the upper limbs. Just think about the centrifugal force generated by your golf swing. This is really pulling the top and bottom parts of the body in different directions. Therefore, strength in your joints is critical in injury prevention.

Some tips for creating a fitness plan that can genuinely improve a game and your overall health include:

1. Don't underestimate the value of strength - While golf isn't necessarily a game of brute strength, muscle development does matter. The stronger a player is, and the better the form, the more distance they are likely to get on drives. To build up the strength it takes to lower one's score, make sure resistance and

weight training are included in an overall golf exercise program.
A player doesn't have to look like a bodybuilder to enjoy a

good game, but stronger arm, back, and leg muscles can make a difference. So, don't overlook building these areas up when putting together your routine. Perhaps as a minimum some press ups or sit ups at home each morning will strengthen your core and upper body.

2. Endurance can help your game - There's nothing more frustrating than getting tired or achy on the back nine and then missing the putt on the 18th to win the match or shoot your best score. To avoid this, make sure endurance training goes into a golfing workout. Basic cardiovascular exercises can help a great deal on this end. You don't have to run 10k every week, for some of you it will simply mean getting off the sofa in the evening and going for a walk, seriously, this will help.

3. Stretching is vital – Nothing can side-line a game faster than a pulled muscle. A fitness routine should include simple stretching exercises to avoid this issue. These exercises should include stretching the back, hamstrings, arms, neck, and so on. Would an athlete run a marathon or 100m sprint without warming up? Therefore, it's not a bad idea to add stretches as

part of a pre-game routine to loosen up before walking up to the first tee.

4. Diet makes a difference - Diet is a part of fitness. Be mindful; it is essential to remember it as part of a golf fitness work- out program. Generally, a well-balanced and healthy diet can make a difference in endurance and ability to play through. If extra weight is causing a problem on the course, dropping a few pounds can help. You might find that losing a few pounds or improving endurance will have benefits in other areas of your life as well.

Chapter 8 - Putt For Dough

The importance of the putter is that about 45% of your score is generated on the green, so spending time focussing on your putting for a beginner is essential. You use your putter more than anything else in your golf bag. If you want to improve your game and hole more putts you will need to make an investment in a well-balanced putter with which you feel comfortable. The putter has a short barrel (or shaft) compared to other clubs. This club head is very heavy so that you can easily hit
the ball in the centre with the desired force. The impact zone is only inclined at a few degrees. This is because on the green we don't want the ball to go up, but just to roll into the hole every time.

There are many different types of golf putter available on the market these days, most of which are slight variations of mallet putter, blade putter or cavity putter.

When selecting a golf putter for yourself you should put into consideration the comfort, feel and the safety that a particular putter offers when playing on the green. You should try to test different types of golf putters before deciding on the best golf one that suits your needs. It's even possible to have a putting lesson with a PGA qualified professional at your local club or golf centre.

Also, on your next purchase, carefully check the shape, length, and weight distribution before buying. If you make the right choice, then you are guaranteed to take many shots off your round and regularly beat your playing partners.

As putting is so vital in improving your golf, I've dedicated the next two chapters to this area of the game.

Chapter 9 - Green Reading

Many golfers dramatically underestimate the value of practicing. Even when we do find time, many golfers just get to the driving range and spend an hour smashing 100 drives as far as they can. One area a golfer should invest more time in is the short game, and in particular, putting. For many this is the least developed skill, and usually the one that causes the biggest negative impact on your scorecard.

The ability to swiftly and accurately read a green, know its pitch, identify its contours, note the direction of the grain, and more will provide the golfer the knowledge needed to make a successful putt every time. If you wish to be a better putter, you'll need to practice this skill and have a routine.

We perform best in a repetitive task when we use a routine. You'll want to develop a green-reading routine to help you putt better more often. Watch the top PGA professionals, they all have a pre-shot routine with their putts.

A routine works to prepare you both physically and mentally to putt, and that preparation allow you to relax - a vital part of a successful putt. This new green reading system will help you make more putts and you'll become increasingly confident. Nothing is better for your putting game than confidence. You will need to come up with a routine that works for you and your style.

However, here is an outline of an exceptional green-reading routine which you can use as a guide:

The Approach: As you walk up to the green, survey the surroundings noting the overall shape, slope, and contours. Make a mental note of the direction of the break for your upcoming putt.

Determine the Distance - Get the distance right. Knowing the distance is critical to great putting. Walk the distance of the putt from the ball to the hole. Make a mental note of how far, much like when you check your yardages on the fairway.

Calculate the Speed - You'll need to determine how much backswing you'll need based on the green speed. Green speeds vary so much, I hesitate to say, but generally, a good guide is one inch of backswing per foot of green. Adjustments must be made for significant elevation changes. Uphill you'll need to add pace while going downhill. You need to take some speed off.

Take a few practice swings to get a feel of the distance required. Know the Break - Most all greens have some amount of break. I like to get far and low behind the ball to see the break. Then I move over to look at the putt from the low side. I want to see both the ball and hole in my field of vision, if possible. Factor in the ball's speed along the putt's line as a slower ball will take more break than a faster one will. Some golfers pick a point on the ground a few inches in front of the ball as the point to aim for, this helps them ensure they set the ball off in along the correct line towards the hole.

Build a Plan - You now have all the information you need to make the putt: distance, speed, and break. Now stand behind the ball one last time and visualize the putt rolling until it falls into the hole. You are teaching your mind what you want your body to do during the putt. Now move into your putting set up and make the putt.

You already know that if you sink more putts, you'll lower your scores and improve your handicap. A well-struck putt will miss the hole every time if not read correctly. Develop your green reading routine and practice well on the putting green. Once you are on the course, that routine will serve you very well every time.

Chapter 10 - Putting Distance Routine

When putting, if you can control the pace correctly, then your distance control will be reasonable. Anyone with perfect distance control will be an impressive putter. Controlling the pace of the golf ball when you are putting is relatively easy - hit it harder to make it go further! But it is much more challenging to realize how hard it is to strike the ball to impart the right amount of speed on the ball which can only come through practice and feedback. For many golfers, judging distance is extremely challenging, get it wrong and you could end up three putting every hole!

The following golf drill tips are crucial to improving your distance control quickly.

Work with three golf balls at the same time to get started.

Set a small target of approximately 6-8 feet away from such as a coin or tee peg.

Set up ready to hit your putt

Close your eyes

Take your stroke

Think to yourself without opening your eyes (this is the key to this golf putting drill) ask yourself, 'Did I hit it too hard, too soft, or just about right? How did it feel?'

Open your eyes. Have you been right as to how hard you hit it? Close your eyes and repeat with the next two balls to correctly regulate your distance. You might feel strange putting with your eyes closed, but there are many top golfers who follow this drill. You must be able to hit three shots in a row with perfect distance control as you repeat this golf putting drill at the same target. You should note how much more you feel the putt in both your hands and your whole body by removing one of your senses. For working on short putts, this is also a good golf trick as it keeps the head from moving.

Now let's make this golf putting drill solidified.

You only have one shot when you are out of the golf course so how can you make this golf putting drill work on the course when you only have a single shot? The clue is to make it harder. To make this drill increasingly harder, carry out the following changes:

Practice with longer putts

Practice with downhill and uphill putts

Practice with curving putts

Lessen the number of balls from three to two and then down to one

Place the three balls around the target at various lengths/types of putt. Then you only have one putt to try and get the distance correct - just as you do when playing out on the course. Like I said earlier, if your distance control on the putting greens is good then you'll be a good putter. You'll be able to turn those three and four putts into two and one putts, considerably improving your score.

Chapter 11 - Golf & Wellbeing

Playing golf is a way to stay healthy, exercise, relax and be outdoors, all at the same time. On the course, we find many benefits for our mind, body, and mental health. Golf & Wellbeing go hand in hand read more to find out.

We all want something that makes us feel good, from physical health to mental well-being. Playing golf game is a great thing to do. In fact, playing golf has proven benefits even to those getting started in golf. Not everyone knows how to reduce daily stress and connect with nature. Read more to find out why.

Benefits of golf to your mental health

1. Increased concentration:

One advantage of Golf is that it allows us to have close contact with nature. Staying at home using smartphones all day has made us forget the healthy habits of the past. Playing golf, can break this habit, calm the body, and make one free from a sedentary lifestyle.

As written above, golf not only trains the body but also the mind. In fact, developing concentration and attention is a prerogative of golf. Golfers tend to notice what is going on around them and try to solve any kind of problem.

The open space and the natural environment around the golf course helps players concentrate, and it also relieves tension, clearing the mind of negative thoughts. Golf helps players become coordinated and flexible. By relaxing the mind, golf increases endurance.

2. Encourages social interaction:

Golf is not a game you should play on your own, in fact most course won't let you play by yourself. Playing with other golfers encourages strong social interactions which are highly beneficial to your mental health. Also, sharing a disastrous round of golf with another person can really strengthen your friendship. Joining a golf club is one of the best ways to meet new people, which is key to keeping your mind alert. This is a key reason that people in retirement choose to join golf clubs, to broaden their circle of friends and meet new people.

3. Helps you sleep better:

If your body doesn't get enough sleep, it won't work well the next day. Lack of sleep has many negative consequences related to physical and mental health. When you don't get

enough sleep, you become forgetful and unbalanced. This increases your risk of stroke or diabetes. When getting started in golf, playing at least two days a week, can improve your mental and physical well-being. It is also useful for reviving sleep, which means that the quality of your sleep will improve.

4. Emotional stability:

Golfers are generally very stable and cope with frustration. It is often difficult to tell whether they are in a good or bad mood. You may not adopt this trait immediately, when you are getting started in golf, but with time you begin to manifest it.

When golfers experience emotions, they use mental techniques to always keep calm. Another character that is notable among golfers is patience.

5. Overcome depression:

Playing golf helps control anxiety and depression. Because it requires high concentration, anxiety has no place.

Those who play golf and practice it, end up learning to relax as well. That is why the medical community is recognizing golf as good therapy.

The practice of golf requires tranquillity, think of the calm required when you to centre yourself over the ball before your shot. For this reason, golfers learn to control their anxiety.

So overall, to end where we began. Golf is an amazing game, for all of the reasons listed above and due to the lifetime of joy you can get from the pursuit of the perfect golf shot. Just re- member to have fun along the way, it's not a good walk spoiled as Mark Twain once said. It's a chance to have fun with friends, in beautiful surroundings, and escape from the distractions of modern life.

Printed in Great Britain
by Amazon